Red Line 5

Vokabellernheft

Ausgabe für Bayern

Herausgeber: Dr. Frank Haß

Ernst Klett Verlag
Stuttgart • Leipzig • Dortmund

Vorwort

Liebe Schülerin, lieber Schüler,

mit diesem Vokabellernheft im praktischen Taschenformat kannst du überall deine Wörter lernen, wiederholen und nachschlagen.
In den Wortlisten kannst du Wörter und Wendungen, die dir schwierig vorkommen, mit Textmarker oder Bleistift markieren, um sie dann immer wieder durchzugehen.
Auch die vielen Übungen nach jedem Lektionsteil unterstützen dich bei der Wiederholung. So kannst du dich prima auf Tests und Prüfungen vorbereiten.
Hinter jedem Wort ist die Lautschrift (z. B. [ɜːθ] für *earth*) angegeben. Diese hilft dir, wenn du nicht weißt, wie du das Wort aussprechen sollst.
Hilfreiche Hinweise zum Umgang mit den Lautschriftzeichen findest du in deinem Englischbuch ab Seite 199 am unteren Rand aller *Dictionary*-Seiten.

Viel Erfolg beim Vokabellernen!

Zoom in – The Commonwealth

p. 8	**organisation** [ˌɔ:gənaɪˈzeɪʃn]	*hier:* Vereinigung; Organisation
	New Zealand [ˌnju: ˈzi:lənd]	Neuseeland
	the Caribbean [ðə ˌkærɪˈbi:ən]	die Karibik
	the Pacific Ocean [ðə pəˌsɪfɪk‿ˈəʊʃn]	der Pazifische Ozean
	recent [ˈri:snt]	kürzlich; neueste; letzte
	head (of state) [ˌhed(‿əv ˈsteɪt)]	(Staats-)Oberhaupt
	monarch [ˈmɒnək]	Monarch; Monarchin
	sporting event [ˈspɔ:tɪŋ‿ɪˌvent]	Sportereignis; Sportveranstaltung
	to **include** [ɪnˈklu:d]	einbeziehen; aufnehmen; einbinden; einschließen
	disability [ˌdɪsəˈbɪləti]	*hier:* Behinderten-; Behinderung; Unfähigkeit
	aim [eɪm]	Ziel; Absicht
	terrorism [ˈterɪzm]	Terrorismus
	threat [θret]	Bedrohung; Gefahr
	development [dɪˈveləpmənt]	Entwicklung
	to **create** [kriˈeɪt]	schaffen; erschaffen; kreieren
	climate change [ˈklaɪmət ˌtʃeɪndʒ]	Klimawandel
	democracy [dɪˈmɒkrəsi]	Demokratie
	human rights *(pl)* [ˌhju:mən ˈraɪts]	Menschenrechte *(Pl.)*
	gender [ˈdʒendə]	Geschlecht(er-)
	to **develop** [dɪˈveləp]	(sich) entwickeln

Ask a friend or a family member to test you on the words you have learned. Then you can practise saying them too!

1 Complete the text.

INTERNET

The Commonwealth

The British ___________ is the head of the Commonwealth. It is an ________________ made up of lots of different countries, including countries on the other side of the world such as Australia and _____ __________. It has many _______, such as fighting for human rights and fighting against ________ ________, but it also organises a __________ __________ every four years called the Commonwealth Games. Anyone who lives in a Commonwealth country can take part, including people with a _______________. In 2020, Maldives became the most _________ country to join the Commonwealth.

2 Match the nouns with their definitions.

1. terrorism
2. monarch
3. threat
4. democracy
5. climate change

a) how the world's weather is changing
b) a violent act for a political purpose
c) people can choose their government
d) something that might cause danger
e) king or queen

Unit 1 Life down under

p. 10	**down under** [ˌdaʊn‿ˈʌndə]	in Australien

Intro

p. 10	**continent** [ˈkɒntɪnənt]	Kontinent; Erdteil
	koala [kəʊˈɑːlə]	Koala
	kangaroo [ˌkæŋgrˈuː]	Känguru
	off [ɒf]	*hier:* vor
	climate [ˈklaɪmət]	Klima
	lifestyle [ˈlaɪfstaɪl]	Lebensart; Lifestyle
p. 11	**Aboriginal people** [æbəˌrɪdʒnl ˈpiːpl]	die Aborigines
	disease [dɪˈziːz]	Krankheit
	to **struggle** [ˈstrʌgl]	kämpfen; ringen; sich anstrengen; Mühe haben
	inadequate [ɪˈnædɪkwət]	unangemessen; unzureichend
	housing [ˈhaʊzɪŋ]	Unterkunft
	proportion [prəˈpɔːʃn]	Anteil
	these days [ˈðiːz ˌdeɪz]	heutzutage
	skilled [skɪld]	qualifiziert; ausgebildet; Fach-
	nurse [nɜːs]	Krankenschwester; Krankenpfleger
	carpenter [ˈkɑːpəntə]	Zimmermann; Zimmerin; Tischler; Tischlerin
	the outback [ði‿ˈaʊtbæk]	Outback *(australisches Hinterland)*
	agriculture *(no pl)* [ˈægrɪkʌltʃə]	Landwirtschaft; Agrikultur
	mining *(no pl)* [ˈmaɪnɪŋ]	Bergbau
	to **contact** [ˈkɒntækt]	sich in Verbindung setzen; kontaktieren
	education [ˌedʒʊˈkeɪʃn]	Ausbildung; Erziehung; Bildung

3 Write the words and find an area in Australia.

1. Australia is one of the largest countries in the world, and it is the only country that is also a _ ☐ _ _ _ _ _ _ _.
2. A person from Australia is an _ ☐ _ _ _ _ _ _ _ _.
3. What do you know about the Australian _ _ _ _ _ ☐ _ _ _?
4. _ ☐ _ _ _ _ _ _ _ _ people have been in Australia for over 50,000 years.
5. British settlers brought _ _ _ _ ☐ _ _ _ to Austrialia in the 18th century.
6. _ _ _ _ ☐ _ _ _ _ _ _ is one of the main industries because there is a lot of land.
7. There are some unusual animals, like the ☐ _ _ _ _, that can only be found in Australia.

The huge area in the centre of Australia is called the '_ _ _ _ _ _ _'.

4 Complete the interview about Australia.

koalas | education | these days | housing | down under | kangaroos | contact

Emma: Hi James, thanks for letting me __________ you. Can I ask you some questions about what it's like __________ __________?

James: Of course!

Emma: What is your favourite thing about Australia?

James: I love the animals. We have __________, which are grey and very cute, and you can sometimes see __________ jumping around too.

Emma: Wow! Can you tell me about the outback?

James: Not many people live there. Children don't get a traditional __________ because there aren't many schools, so they go to the School of the Air. But __________ __________, there is a lot more tourism.

Emma: Interesting. I'd like to know a bit about Aboriginal life too.

James: It can be very hard. Many people live in inadequate __________ and struggle for their rights.

Topic 1

p. 12	to **be used to** *(+ -ing)* [bi ˈjuːst tə]	gewöhnt sein an
	knowledge *(no pl)* [ˈnɒlɪdʒ]	Wissen; Kenntnisse
	to **affect** [əˈfekt]	beeinflussen; beeinträchtigen; betreffen
	daily [ˈdeɪli]	täglich
	sense of community [ˌsens‿əv kəˈmjuːnəti]	Gemeinschaftsgefühl
	to **look out for** [ˌlʊk‿ˈaʊt fə]	*hier:* aufpassen auf
	responsible (for) [rɪsˈpɒnsəbl (fə)]	verantwortlich (für); verantwortungsvoll
	to **bring up** [ˌbrɪŋ‿ˈʌp]	aufziehen; großziehen
	to **raise** [reɪz]	*hier:* aufziehen; großziehen; hissen *(Flagge)*
	point of view [ˌpɔɪnt‿əv ˈvjuː]	Standpunkt; Perspektive
	respectful [rɪˈspektfl]	respektvoll
	common [ˈkɒmən]	gemeinsam; üblich; gewöhnlich; (weit) verbreitet; gebräuchlich
	respect [rɪˈspekt]	Respekt
	to **look up** [ˌlʊk‿ˈʌp]	*hier:* aufschauen
	to **pass on** [ˌpɑːs‿ˈɒn]	weitergeben
	giant [dʒaɪənt]	Riesen-; riesig
	creature [ˈkriːtʃə]	Kreatur; Lebewesen; Geschöpf
	plant [plɑːnt]	Pflanze
	connection [kəˈnekʃn]	Verbindung
	meaning [ˈmiːnɪŋ]	Bedeutung
	sacred [ˈseɪkrɪd]	heilig
	to **make a fuss** [ˌmeɪk‿ə ˈfʌs]	einen Aufstand machen; viel Aufhebens machen
	behaviour [bɪˈheɪvjə]	Verhalten
	to **accept** [əkˈsept]	akzeptieren; annehmen; hinnehmen
	belief [bɪˈliːf]	Glaube; Überzeugung
p. 13	**ignorant** [ˈɪgnərənt]	ignorant; unwissend

	to **ignore** [ɪg'nɔ:]	ignorieren; außer Acht lassen
	politeness [pə'laɪtnəs]	Höflichkeit
	to **tolerate** ['tɒlreɪt]	tolerieren; dulden
	rudeness ['ru:dnəs]	Unhöflichkeit; Unverschämtheit
	acceptable [ək'septəbl]	akzeptabel; annehmbar
	tolerance ['tɒlrns]	Toleranz
p. 14	**nomadic** [nə'mædɪk]	nicht sesshaft
	to **hunt** [hʌnt]	jagen
	to **communicate** [kə'mju:nɪkeɪt]	kommunizieren; sich verständigen
	air conditioning *(no pl)* ['eəkən,dɪʃnɪŋ]	Klimaanlage
p. 15	**decoration** [,dek'reɪʃn]	Dekoration
	to **plant** [plɑ:nt]	pflanzen
	to **survive** [sə'vaɪv]	überleben
	lady ['leɪdi]	Dame; Frau

5 Match the sentence parts.

1. She brought	a) a fuss all the time.
2. I am used	b) up my children.
3. We look	c) out for each other.
4. My mother passed	d) to Aboriginal traditions.
5. He makes	e) on lots of information to me.

6 Find eight adjectives.

R	G	W	E	S	A	C	R	E	D
I	I	F	M	K	V	P	O	N	A
G	A	O	J	I	H	J	A	W	I
N	N	H	E	L	U	B	N	I	L
O	T	B	X	L	D	O	T	S	Y
R	E	S	P	E	C	T	F	U	L
A	Y	N	T	D	R	L	E	M	R
N	O	M	A	D	I	C	T	A	C
T	V	U	K	F	A	V	Q	E	G
P	A	D	C	O	M	M	O	N	Y

1. ______________________ 5. ______________________

2. ______________________ 6. ______________________

3. ______________________ 7. ______________________

4. ______________________ 8. ______________________

7 Write the words in English.

1.  ______________________

2.  ______________________

3.  ______________________

4.  ______________________

8 Complete Koa's text with words from the same word family.

1. I want to share my ____________________ (know) about the Aboriginals.
2. We are ____________________ (respect) towards older people.
3. The Aboriginals have a ____________________ (connect) with the land and its animals and plants.
4. We want the tourists to change their ____________________ (behave) and show respect for our land.
5. Everyone should learn to ____________________ (tolerance) different traditions because Australians have lots of different ____________________ (believe).
6. People can't ____________________ (ignorant) the Aboriginals' human rights.
7. We Aboriginals have a strong sense of community, and we all ____________________ (acceptable) each other as we are.

Topic 2

p. 19	**frightened** ['fraɪtnd]	verängstigt
	brilliant ['brɪliənt]	toll; brillant; strahlend
	to **gleam** [gli:m]	schimmern
	cluster ['klʌstə]	Klumpen; Anhäufung
	seashell ['si:ʃel]	Muschel
	Aussie *(infml)* ['ɒzi]	Australier; Australierin; australisch
	coat hanger ['kəʊt ˌhæŋə]	Kleiderbügel
	incredible [ɪn'kredɪbl]	unglaublich
	to **mention** ['menʃn]	erwähnen
	Indonesia [ˌɪndə'ni:ʒə]	Indonesien
	to **get itchy feet** [get‿ˌɪtʃi 'fi:t]	Fernweh haben; es irgendwo nicht mehr aushalten
	trip [trɪp]	*hier:* Reise
	speaking of sb/sth ['spi:kɪŋ‿əv]	apropos; da wir gerade von jmdm./etw. sprechen
	loads (of) *(infml)* [ləʊdz (əv)]	jede Menge; massenhaft
	to **depend (on)** [dɪ'pend (ɒn)]	abhängen (von)
	harbour ['hɑ:bə]	Hafen
	honest ['ɒnɪst]	ehrlich
	left [left]	übrig
	to **walk by** [ˌwɔ:k 'baɪ]	vorbeilaufen
	laid-back [ˌleɪd'bæk]	entspannt; locker
	mate [meɪt]	Kumpel; Kamerad; Kameradin
	barbie *(Aus) (infml)* ['bɑ:bi]	Grill(party)
	by [baɪ]	bei; an
	No way! [ˌnəʊ 'weɪ]	*hier:* Ich glaub's nicht!; Auf keinen Fall!
p. 20	**self-confident** [ˌself'kɒnfɪdnt]	selbstsicher; selbstbewusst
	jealous ['dʒeləs]	eifersüchtig; neidisch
	to **work out** [ˌwɜ:k‿'aʊt]	*hier:* sich entwickeln; herausbekommen
p. 21	to **put on** [ˌpʊt‿'ɒn]	*hier:* auftragen

9 Find the words and complete the messages.

Dave: Hey Chris! Jess m_ _ _ _ _ _ _ _ that you're in Sydney – I'm here as well!

Chris: N_ w_ _! Let's meet up – I want to experience the A_ _ _ _ _ lifestyle ☺.

Dave: There are l_ _ _ _ o_ exciting things to do here. For example, people often organise b_ _ _ _ _ _ on the beach.

Christ: That's cool! S_ _ _ _ _ _ _ o_ food, I'm quite hungry …

Dave: Me too! Let's go to the harbour for lunch. I'll introduce you to my m_ _ _ _.

10 Complete the table with the words.

laid-back trip mention communicate harbour brilliant gleam honest jealous seashell depend decoration

Nouns	Verbs	Adjectives

11 Put the verbs in the right sentences.

work out | pass on | look up | put on | walk by

1. If you ________________ to the sky, you can see a rainbow.
2. How did the new project ________________ for you?
3. You should ________________ this information to your parents.
4. Let's ________________ the museum tomorrow to see how expensive it is.
5. Aren't you going to ________________ a coat? It's so cold!

12 Which is the odd one out?

1. incredible • coral • self-confident • responsible
2. turtle • creature • koala • kangaroo
3. affect • left • raise • survive
4. rudeness • tolerance • politeness • honest

13 Write the words and find a country in Asia.

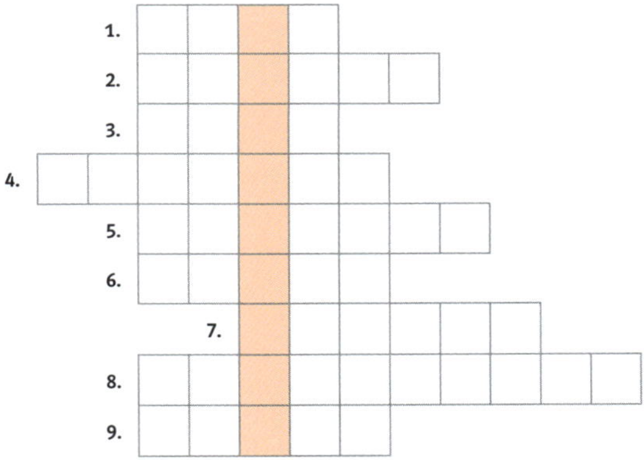

1. When you go on a …, you travel somewhere.
2. If you are …, you tell the truth.
3. Another word for a woman is a … .
4. A … is a place on the coast where ships arrive and leave.
5. To … something is to say it without giving much detail.
6. When seashells …, they shine very brightly.
7. … means religious and holy.
8. If you think something is scary, you feel … .
9. When you … something, you put it in the ground to make it grow.

_ _ _ _ _ _ _ _ _ is a country in Asia.

Text 2

p. 23	**wonder** ['wʌndə]	Wunder
	earth [ɜ:θ]	die Erde; Boden; Erdboden
	underwater [ˌʌndə'wɔ:tə]	Unterwasser-
	reef [ri:f]	Riff
	to **stretch** [stretʃ]	sich strecken; erstrecken; dehnen
	ecosystem ['i:kəʊˌsɪstəm]	Ökosystem
	coral ['kɒrəl]	Koralle
	turtle ['tɜ:tl]	Schildkröte
	bleaching ['bli:tʃɪŋ]	Bleichen; Ausbleichen
	stress [stres]	*hier:* Stress; Betonung
	alga *(sg)* ['ælgə], **algae** *(pl)* ['ældʒi:]	Alge
	snorkelling *(BE)* ['snɔ:klɪŋ]	Schnorcheln
	platform ['plætfɔ:m]	Plattform; Bahnsteig
	waste [weɪst]	*hier:* Exkremente; Abfall
	to **pollute** [pə'lu:t]	verschmutzen; verunreinigen
	oil spill ['ɔɪl ˌspɪl]	Ölteppich
	destination [ˌdestɪ'neɪʃn]	Ziel; Reiseziel
	outside [ˌaʊt'saɪd]	*hier:* außerhalb
	lane [leɪn]	*hier:* Fahrspur; Weg; Gasse
	to **recover** [rɪ'kʌvə]	sich erholen
p. 24	**government** ['gʌvnmənt]	Regierung
	to **repair** [rɪ'peə]	reparieren
	solution [sə'lu:ʃn]	Lösung
	consequence ['kɒnsɪkwəns]	Konsequenz; Folge; Auswirkung

14 Write the words in English.

1.  ____________________

2.  ____________________

3. 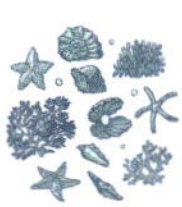 ____________________

15 Complete the text.

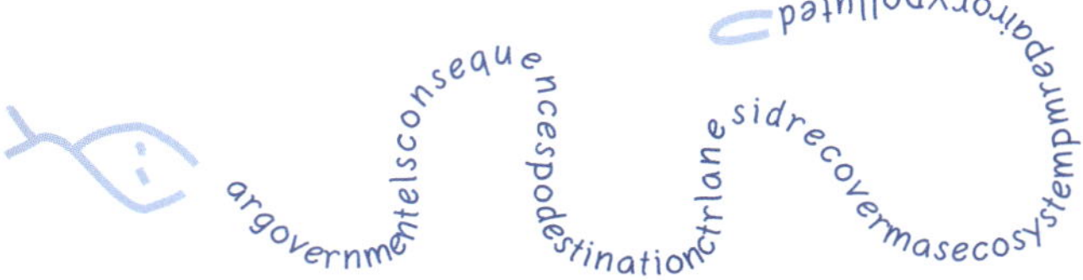

Evening News

Oil spill in Great Barrier Reef

It is one of the worst oil spills the Great Barrier Reef has ever seen! The reef is a popular tourist ______________, but terrible things can happen too. Ships should use official ______________, but one Chinese ship did not follow the rules. The reef was hit, and there were many serious ______________ for the captain and the reef. It will be difficult to ______________ the reef that was damaged; some areas may even never ______________. The sea has been ______________ by the oil, and hundreds of species of plants and animals are gone. The ______________ of the reef will never be the same again. What will the ______________ do to save the reef?

16 Find the nouns and complete the definitions.

a) Find eight nouns.

E	G	O	V	E	R	N	M	E	N	T	W
R	W	G	J	A	F	T	I	H	I	D	A
P	U	I	N	R	O	Y	W	G	L	V	T
O	D	E	S	T	I	N	A	T	I	O	N
M	F	B	T	H	W	K	S	E	R	C	E
T	A	E	R	P	L	A	T	F	O	R	M
S	V	C	E	H	A	P	E	A	D	Y	U
C	O	N	S	E	Q	U	E	N	C	E	M
E	C	O	S	Y	S	T	E	M	K	O	X

b) Complete the definitions with the right nouns.

1. The group of people who lead a country are the … .
2. A community of animals and plants is an … .
3. Things or materials that you don't want anymore are … .
4. The place where passengers get on and off trains is a … .
5. The result of an action is a … .
6. The place where you want to go is your … .
7. Another word for world is … .
8. Being worried or nervous is … .

Unit 2 The world of work

Intro

p. 32	**hairdressing salon** ['heəˌdresɪŋ ˌsælɒn]	Friseursalon
	apprentice [ə'prentɪs]	Lehrling; Auszubildender; Auszubildende
	to **work one's way up** [ˌwɜ:k wʌnz ˌweɪ‿'ʌp]	sich hocharbeiten
	(hair) stylist [('heə) ˌstaɪlɪst]	Friseur; Friseurin
	tiring ['taɪrɪŋ]	ermüdend
p. 33	**travel agent** ['trævl‿ˌeɪdʒnt]	Reisebürokaufmann; Reisebürokauffrau
	agency ['eɪdʒnsi]	*hier:* Büro; Agentur
	to **specialise (in)** [ˌspeʃlaɪz(‿'ɪn)]	sich spezialisieren (auf)
	advantage [əd'vɑ:ntɪdʒ]	Vorteil
	shift [ʃɪft]	Schicht
	to **be understanding** [bi‿ˌʌndə'stændɪŋ]	verständnisvoll sein
	chef [ʃef]	Koch; Köchin
	colleague ['kɒli:g]	Kollege; Kollegin
p. 32	**workplace** ['wɜ:kpleɪs]	Arbeitsplatz; Arbeitsstätte
p. 33	to **reserve** [rɪ'zɜ:v]	reservieren; vorbestellen
	included [ɪn'klu:dɪd]	inbegriffen

Highlight the words in the vocabulary list that you find more difficult and practise them more. Each time you practise, you should know more words!

1 Find the jobs and where the person works.

a) Find the jobs.

1. ______________________
2. ______________________
3. ______________________
4. ______________________

b) Find where the person works.

1. A ______________________ works in a r_ _ _ _ _ _ _ _ _.
2. A ______________________ works in an a_ _ _ _ _.
3. A ______________________ works in a s_ _ _ _.
4. A ______________________ works in a h_ _ _ _ _ _ _.

2 Which is the odd one out?

1. specialise • reserve • apprentice • stretch
2. chef • workplace • travel agent • stylist
3. hard-working • shift • understanding • determined
4. consequence • advantage • business trip • tiring
5. travel agent • trip • destination • ecosystem

3 Complete the blog.

colleagues | advantages | shifts | understanding | specialise | agent | workplace | tiring | work

BLOG

My first day at work

Today was my first day as a travel ________________, and I really enjoyed it! My new ________________ were all nice to me and were very ________________ when I made mistakes. I learned a lot about the agency. After two years, I will be able to ________________ in one part of the world if I want to. I can't wait to ________________ my way up in the company! The first day was very ________________ because I did not get many breaks and I had to talk to customers. I really like the ________________ because it is very colourful and there are lots of pictures of travel destinations. One of the ________________ of working at this company is that I can get free holidays! I have to make sure that I do enough ________________ to get those though.

Topic 1

p. 34	**interest (in)** ['ɪntrəst (ɪn)]	Interesse
	photography [fə'tɒgrəfi]	Fotografie
	requirement [rɪ'kwaɪəmənt]	Voraussetzung; Anforderung
	to **have an eye for detail** [ˌhæv‿ən‿ˌaɪ fə 'di:teɪl]	einen Blick fürs Detail haben
	on one's own [ˌɒn wʌnz‿'əʊn]	allein; für sich
	CV (= curriculum vitae) [ˌsi:'vi: (kəˌrɪkjələm 'vi:taɪ)]	Lebenslauf
	to **apply (for)** [ə'plaɪ (fə)]	sich bewerben (für/um)
	electrician [ˌelɪk'trɪʃn]	Elektriker; Elektrikerin
	neither ['naɪðə]	auch nicht; keiner von beiden
	repair [rɪ'peə]	Reparatur(arbeit)
	installation [ˌɪnstə'leɪʃn]	Aufstellen; Installation; Verlegung; Anschluss
	driving licence *(BE)* ['draɪvɪŋ ˌlaɪsns]	Führerschein
	to **be prepared to do sth** [bi: prɪˌpeəd‿tə 'du:]	bereit sein, etw. zu tun
	additionally [ə'dɪʃnli]	außerdem; zusätzlich
	grade [greɪd]	*hier:* Note; Klasse
	GCSE (= General Certificate of Secondary Education) [ˌdʒi:si:es'i: (ˌdʒenrl səˌtɪfɪkət‿əv ˌsekəndri‿edʒʊ'keɪʃn)]	*allg. Abschluss der weiterführenden Schulen in GB*
	salary ['sælri]	Gehalt
	on-the-job training [ˌɒnðədʒɒb 'treɪnɪŋ]	Ausbildung am Arbeitsplatz
	once [wʌns]	sobald; wenn; als
	qualification [ˌkwɒlɪfɪ'keɪʃn]	Qualifikation; Abschluss; Schulabschluss
	to **progress** [prə'gres]	vorankommen
	marketing *(no pl)* ['mɑ:kɪtɪŋ]	Marketing; Vermarktung; Vertrieb
	excellent ['ekslnt]	exzellent; hervorragend

	communication [kəˌmjuːnɪˈkeɪʃn]	Kommunikation(s-)
	smart appearance [ˌsmɑːt‿əˈpɪərns]	gepflegtes Erscheinungsbild
p. 35	**male** [meɪl]	männlich
	strength [streŋθ]	Stärke; Kraft
	practical [ˈpræktɪkl]	praktisch (veranlagt)
	to **prioritise** [praɪˈɒrɪtaɪz]	vorrangig behandeln
	customer service [ˌkʌstəmə ˈsɜːvɪs]	Kundendienst; Kundenbetreuung
	So do I. [ˌsəʊ du‿ˈaɪ]	Ich auch.
	neither … nor … [ˈnaɪðə … nɔː]	weder … noch …
	nor [nɔː]	und auch nicht; noch
	not … either [nɒt … ˈaɪðə]	auch nicht
p. 36	**job title** [ˈdʒɒb ˌtaɪtl]	Stellenbezeichnung; Berufsbezeichnung
	business trip [ˈbɪznɪs ˌtrɪp]	Geschäftsreise
	abroad [əˈbrɔːd]	im Ausland; ins Ausland
	On the one hand …, (but) on the other hand … [ɒn ðə‿ˈwʌn ˌhænd … (bʌt‿) ɒn ði‿ˈʌðə ˌhænd …]	Einerseits …, (aber) andererseits …

4 Complete the job advert.

Wanted: Apprentice Photographer

We are looking for an *ex*_ _ _ _ _ _ _ photographer to help us with our new project in Sydney.

You should be *pr*_ _ _ _ _ _ to work hard, but you will *pr*_ _ _ _ _ _ quickly in the company.

We offer a great *sa*_ _ _ _, a friendly workplace and opportunities to go *ab*_ _ _ _ to work in other countries.

There are also some *re*_ _ _ _ _ _ _ _ _ _ that you must have. You must have some experience with *ph*_ _ _ _ _ _ _ _ _ equipment, an eye for *de*_ _ _ _ and good GCSE *gr*_ _ _ _.

It would be good if you had a *dr*_ _ _ _ _ *li*_ _ _ _ _ too, so that you can travel around by yourself.

Send us your CV to *ap*_ _ _ for this job.

5 Match the words that mean the same.

1. grade	a) improve
2. once	b) incredible
3. prepared	c) when
4. make progress	d) mark
5. excellent	e) also
6. additionally	f) ready

6 Match the words with their definitions.

1. prioritise	a) When you pass an exam, you get a … .
2. marketing	b) If you are …, you are good at being active and working with your hands.
3. practical	c) … means sharing information with a person or people.
4. qualification	d) If you … something, you treat it as very important.
5. communication	e) … means selling a product, often through adverts.

Topic 2

p. 40	**application** [ˌæplɪ'keɪʃn]	Bewerbung; Anwendung
	Dear ..., [dɪə]	*hier:* Sehr geehrte(r) ..., *(Anrede in Briefen)*
	advert (= advertisement) ['ædvɜːt (əd'vɜːtɪsmənt)]	Anzeige; Werbespot
	apprenticeship [ə'prentɪʃɪp]	Ausbildung; Lehre
	DIY shop [ˌdiːaɪ'waɪ ˌʃɒp]	Baumarkt
	to **volunteer** [ˌvɒlən'tɪə]	*hier:* ehrenamtlich arbeiten; sich freiwillig melden
	the elderly *(no pl)* [ðiˌ'eldəli]	ältere Menschen; Senioren
	everyday ['evrideɪ]	alltäglich
	hard-working [ˌhɑːd'wɜːkɪŋ]	fleißig
	determined [dɪ'tɜːmɪnd]	(fest) entschlossen; entschieden; zielstrebig
	deaf [def]	gehörlos; schwerhörig; taub
	despite [dɪ'spaɪt]	trotz
	hearing aid ['hɪərɪŋˌeɪd]	Hörgerät
	piano [pi'ænəʊ]	Klavier; Piano
	to **pass** [pɑːs]	*hier:* bestehen; vorbeigehen; durchgehen
	qualified ['kwɒlɪfaɪd]	qualifiziert
	attached [ə'tætʃt]	angefügt; angehängt
	Yours sincerely, [ˌjɔːz sɪn'sɪəli]	Mit freundlichen Grüßen
	date of birth [ˌdeɪtˌəv 'bɜːθ]	Geburtsdatum
	secondary school ['sekəndri ˌskuːl]	weiterführende Schule
	advanced [əd'vɑːnst]	fortgeschritten
	intermediate [ɪntə'miːdiət]	Mittel-; mittleres Niveau
	to **type** [taɪp]	tippen
	reference ['refrns]	Referenz; Empfehlungsschreiben; Bezug
p. 41	to **prepare** [prɪ'peə]	vorbereiten; zubereiten
	letter of application [ˌletərˌəvˌæplɪ'keɪʃn]	Bewerbungsbrief
	confident ['kɒnfɪdnt]	zuversichtlich; selbstsicher

	job interview [ˈdʒɒb ˈɪntəvjuː]	Vorstellungsgespräch
	duck [dʌk]	Ente
p. 42	**Hold the line, please.** [ˌhəʊld ðə ˈlaɪn]	Bleiben Sie bitte am Apparat.
	electronics *(no pl)* [ˌelekˈtrɒnɪks]	Elektronik
p. 43	**surgeon** [ˈsɜːdʒn]	Chirurg; Chirurgin
	pilot [ˈpaɪlət]	Pilot; Pilotin

7 Complete the job application.

MAIL

Dear Mrs Jones,

I am writing to apply for the ________________ at your office. I saw your ________________ online and I believe I am the best person for the job.

As you can see in my ________________, I am very creative. I like to draw and I also play the piano; sometimes I even play for my grandparents.

I also ________________ for a month in a photograhy shop. I helped to plan events and I ________________ letters to customers. I feel that I am very ________________ for the job, and I hope that you agree. I look forward to hearing from you.

Yours ________________,

Ellen Anderson

8 Find eight adjectives.

D	A	T	C	G	U	I	T	D	S	D	A
E	F	G	O	U	L	C	M	E	B	H	T
Q	B	I	N	J	O	S	E	T	L	E	T
U	U	O	F	P	R	C	D	E	A	F	A
A	S	V	I	Y	S	A	A	R	O	N	C
L	A	P	D	A	C	J	F	M	N	I	H
I	N	T	E	R	M	E	D	I	A	T	E
F	I	W	N	A	D	V	A	N	C	E	D
I	T	K	T	G	E	Y	V	E	D	O	T
E	V	E	R	Y	D	A	Y	D	P	A	W
D	H	I	B	V	U	B	K	I	T	X	A

1. ______________________ 5. ______________________

2. ______________________ 6. ______________________

3. ______________________ 7. ______________________

4. ______________________ 8. ______________________

9 What can you see in the pictures?

1.  ______________________

2.  ______________________

3.  ______________________

4.  ______________________

10 Complete the conversation.

Teacher: Hi Thomas, how can I help you today?

Thomas: Hi Mrs Williams! I'm writing a CV and a l_ _ _ _ _ of a_ _ _ _ _ _ _ _ _ _ for a job. Please can I write your name as a r_ _ _ _ _ _ _ _?

Teacher: Of course! I would be very happy to write about you. You are very h_ _ _-w_ _ _ _ _ _ and I hope you get the job. What are you a_ _ _ _ _ _ _ for?

Thomas: Thank you so much! I want to be an apprentice electrician. I'd be helping with r_ _ _ _ _ _ in people's houses.

Teacher: That sounds great, Thomas. Do you know which q_ _ _ _ _ _ _ _ _ _ _ _ _ you need?

Thomas: Yes, I need at least a GCSE g_ _ _ _ 5 in English and Maths.

Teacher: You have been doing so well at s_ _ _ _ _ _ _ _ school. I'm sure they will invite you for a job i_ _ _ _ _ _ _ _.

Thomas: Thank you, I hope so too!

Text 2

p. 44	**matter** [ˈmætə]	Angelegenheit; Frage
	bank balance *(no pl)* [ˈbæŋk ˌbæləns]	Kontostand
	mistake [mɪˈsteɪk]	Fehler
	income tax [ˈɪnkʌm ˌtæks]	Einkommenssteuer
	to **treat oneself to sth** [ˈtriːt ˌwʌnself tə]	sich etw. gönnen
	pair [peə]	Paar
	sensible [ˈsensəbl]	vernünftig
	useful [ˈjuːsfl]	nützlich; hilfreich
	gaming [ˈgeɪmɪŋ]	Computerspiele-
	to **employ** [ɪmˈplɔɪ]	einstellen; anstellen; beschäftigen
	billionaire [ˌbɪljəˈneə]	Milliardär; Milliardärin
	frugal [ˈfruːgl]	sparsam; genügsam
	to **give away** [ˌgɪv‿əˈweɪ]	verschenken
	happiness [ˈhæpɪnəs]	Glück; Zufriedenheit; Fröhlichkeit
p. 45	**physical** [ˈfɪzɪkl]	physisch; körperlich
	coin [kɔɪn]	Münze
	to **exchange** [ɪksˈtʃeɪndʒ]	tauschen; austauschen
	grain [greɪn]	Korn; Getreide
	currency [ˈkʌrnsi]	Währung
	throughout [θruˈaʊt]	während; über; durchgehend
	China [ˈtʃaɪnə]	China
	trading [ˈtreɪdɪŋ]	Handel
	to **increase** [ɪnˈkriːs]	zunehmen; vergrößern; erhöhen; steigern
	Middle Ages [ˌmɪdl‿ˈeɪdʒɪz]	Mittelalter
	stock exchange [ˈstɒk‿ɪksˌtʃeɪndʒ]	(Wertpapier-)Börse
	share [ʃeə]	(An)teil; Aktie
	to **invest** [ɪnˈvest]	investieren
	value [ˈvæljuː]	Wert; Wertvorstellung

	introduction [ˌɪntrəˈdʌkʃn]	Einleitung; Einführung; Vorstellung
	credit card [ˈkredɪt ˌkɑːd]	Kreditkarte
	secure [sɪˈkjʊə]	sicher
	debt [det]	Schuld(en)
	to **pay off** [ˌpeɪ‿ˈɒf]	abbezahlen; ausbezahlen
	that [ðæt]	so *(Betonung)*
	to **make sure** [ˌmeɪk ˈʃɔː]	dafür sorgen; darauf achten
	digital [ˈdɪdʒɪtl]	digital
	payment [ˈpeɪmənt]	Zahlung; Bezahlung
	cryptocurrency [ˈkrɪptəˌkʌrənsi]	Kryptowährung *(digitales Zahlungsmittel)*
	virtual [ˈvɜːtʃuəl]	virtuell *(vom Computer simuliert)*
	certain [ˈsɜːtn]	sicher; gewiss
	mint [mɪnt]	Münzanstalt
	Iceland [ˈaɪslənd]	Island
	even though [ˌiːvn ˈðəʊ]	auch wenn; obwohl
p. 46	**secret** [ˈsiːkrət]	Geheimnis
	fool [fuːl]	Narr; Dummkopf
	parted [ˈpɑːrtɪd]	getrennt
	evil [ˈiːvl]	das Böse

11 Match the opposites.

1. employed	a) together
2. sensible	b) silly
3. parted	c) good
4. coin	d) fired
5. evil	e) note

12 Find the words.

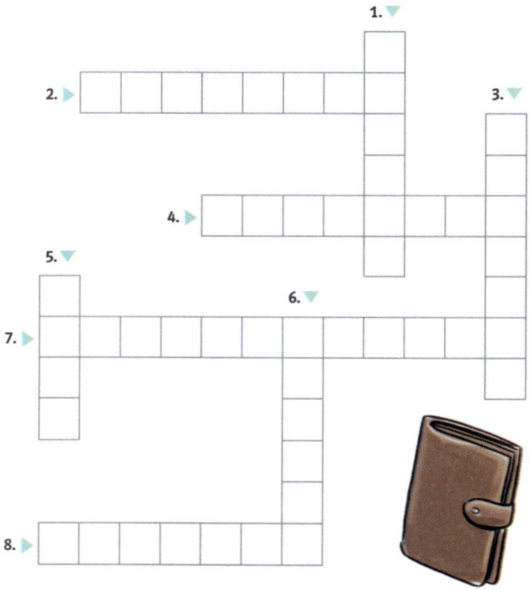

▼
1. A … is something you can't tell others.
3. When you use money to buy something, you make a … .
5. A … is where money is made.
6. If something is … , it helps you in different ways.

▶
2. To … something means to give something away and get something in return.
4. The … is the type of money used in a country.
7. An … is something you write at the beginning of a text.
8. A … image is created by a computer.

13 Complete Eva's diary.

secure | make sure | fool | currency | coins
balance | credit card | payment | treat

Monday, 25th June

I have just started my holiday in France – what a terrible day! Yesterday, when I arrived, I realised that I forgot to exchange the ______________ from pounds to euros! So I had to run to a bank. Then I dropped my ______________ everywhere on the street, it was so embarrassing. When I got home, I could not find my ______________ ______________ anywhere. Oh no! I left it in the supermarket where I was making a ______________. I have to go back tomorrow to find it, but I hope it is ______________ until then. Today, I checked my bank ______________ to ______________ ______________ that I had enough money. Only 20 euros left! I did not have enough money to ______________ myself on holiday. I am such a ______________!

Unit 3 Our digital lives

Intro

p. 54	**human** ['hju:mən]	Mensch; menschlich
	either … or … ['aɪðə … ɔ: …]	entweder … oder …
	one another [ˌwʌn‿ə'nʌðə]	einander; gegenseitig
	hieroglyph ['haɪrəglɪf]	Hieroglyphe *(Bilderschriftzeichen)*
	to **date back (to)** [ˌdeɪt 'bæk tʊ]	datieren (aus); stammen (aus)
	temple ['templ]	Tempel(-)
	tomb [tu:m]	Grab; Gruft
	ancient ['eɪnʃnt]	alt; altertümlich
	Egypt ['i:dʒɪpt]	Ägypten
	to **represent** [ˌreprɪ'zent]	repräsentieren; stehen für; darstellen
	emoji [ɪ'məʊdʒi]	Emoji *(grafisches Symbol)*
	to **shorten** ['ʃɔ:tn]	verkürzen; kürzen
	to **express** [ɪk'spres]	ausdrücken
	printing press ['prɪntɪŋ ˌpres]	Druckerpresse
	to **copy** ['kɒpi]	kopieren; abschreiben
	to **spread** [spred]	*hier:* (sich) verbreiten
	to **publish** ['pʌblɪʃ]	veröffentlichen; publizieren; verlegen
p. 55	**homing pigeon** ['həʊmɪŋ ˌpɪdʒən]	Brieftaube
	to **carry** ['kæri]	*hier:* befördern
	war [wɔ:]	Krieg
	to **award sb sth** [ə'wɔ:d]	jmdm. etw. verleihen
	medal ['medl]	Medaille
	sign language ['saɪn ˌlæŋgwɪdʒ]	Gebärdensprache; Zeichensprache

lip [lɪp] — Lippe(n-)
transatlantic [ˌtrænzət'læntɪk] — transatlantisch
to **revolutionise** [ˌrevl'uːʃnaɪz] — revolutionieren
to **inform** [ɪn'fɔːm] — informieren
crisis *(sg)* ['kraɪsɪs], **crises** *(pl)* ['kraɪsiːz] — Krise

1 Write the verbs in the right form in the sentences.

publish | represent | revolutionise | spread | carry

1. Communication has been ______________ by computers.
2. Information is quickly ______________ online.
3. Words and sounds can be ______________ by symbols.
4. Messages were ______________ by homing pigeons in the war.
5. Lots of books are now ______________ online.

2 What are the words in English?

1.  ______________
2.  ______________
3.  ______________
4.  ______________

3 Write the words and find an ancient way of communicating.

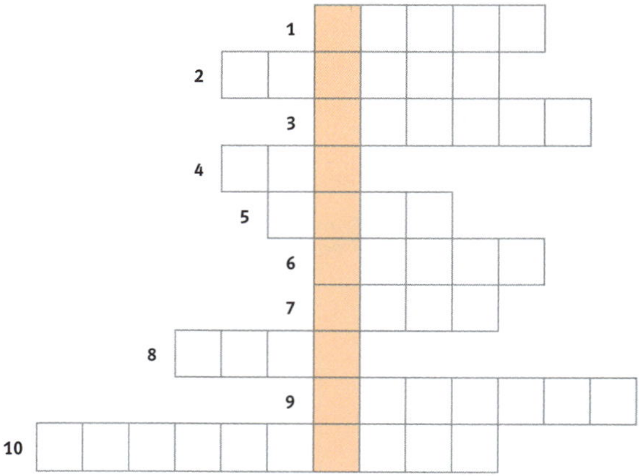

1. … is another word for man or person.
2. A time of danger or emergency is a … .
3. People use … to shorten messages and express feelings.
4. A … is often a fight between different countries.
5. In the past, important people were put in a … when they died.
6. … used to be a type of currency before money.
7. When you kiss someone, you use your … .
8. When you … something, you repeat it exactly the same.
9. When you prepare a book for sale, you … it.
10. Most people check their phone lots of times… the day.

An ancient way of communicating was using a

_ _ _ _ _ _ _ _ _ _.

Topic 1

p. 56	to **be about to do sth** [bi‿ə'baʊt‿tə]	im Begriff sein, etw. zu tun
	to **message** ['mesɪdʒ]	eine Nachricht senden
	to **get on** [ˌget‿'ɒn]	miteinander auskommen
	double Physics [ˌdʌbl 'fɪzɪks]	Doppelstunde Physik
	(a) couple of [ə 'kʌpl‿əv]	(ein) paar
	to **point** [pɔɪnt]	zeigen
	to **go red** [ˌgəʊ 'red]	rot werden
	to **storm** [stɔ:m]	stürmen
	to **be sorry** [bi: 'sɒri]	leidtun
	to **leave sb alone** [ˌli:v‿ə'ləʊn]	jmdn. in Ruhe lassen
	to **run off** [ˌrʌn‿'ɒf]	(plötzlich) weggehen; abhauen
	apparently [ə'pærntli]	offensichtlich; anscheinend
	afterwards ['ɑ:ftəwədz]	danach; hinterher
	to **forgive** [fə'gɪv]	vergeben; verzeihen
	conflict ['kɒnflɪkt]	Auseinandersetzung; Konflikt
	complicated ['kɒmplɪkeɪtɪd]	kompliziert
	to **do without sth** [ˌdu: wɪ'ðaʊt]	ohne etw. auskommen
	to **text** [tekst]	eine Textnachricht schreiben
	to **take sb's side** [ˌteɪk ˌsʌmbədiz‿'saɪd]	auf jmds. Seite stehen
p. 57	to **keep up (with)** [ˌki:p‿'ʌp (wɪð)]	*hier:* auf dem Laufenden sein (über); mithalten (mit)
	affair [ə'feə]	Affäre; Sache; Angelegenheit
	cyberbullying ['saɪbəˌbʊliɪŋ]	Cyber-Mobbing
p. 58	to **block** [blɒk]	blockieren; verstellen
	to **mess up** [ˌmes‿'ʌp]	verpfuschen; in Unordnung bringen
	misunderstanding [ˌmɪsʌndə'stændɪŋ]	Missverständnis
	on purpose [ɒn 'pɜ:pəs]	absichtlich
	text message ['tekst ˌmesɪdʒ]	Textnachricht
	account [ə'kaʊnt]	Konto; Account
	to **delete** [dɪ'li:t]	löschen
p. 59	**understandably** [ˌʌndə'stændəbli]	verständlicherweise

4 Match the sentence parts.

1. I keep	a) alone when I am angry.
2. I take	b) up with all my friends' information.
3. I get	c) without my phone.
4. He leaves me	d) my mother's side in the argument.
5. I can't do	e) up my sister's bedroom.
6. I often mess	f) on with my new neighbour.

5 Complete the table with the words.

conflict · transatlantic · misunderstanding · shorten · delete · complicated · forgive · affair · inform · certain · account · ancient

Nouns	Verbs	Adjectives

6 Complete the conversation.

Sophie: Hey Hannah, I sent you a m_ _ _ _ _ _ yesterday but you didn't message me back. Are you okay?

Hannah: Sorry Sophie! I forgot to tell you, I actually deleted my a_ _ _ _ _ _.

Sophie: Oh really? Was that o_ p_ _ _ _ _ _ _ or by accident?

Hannah: Haha, it wasn't by accident. I think that I spend too much time on social media.

I can d_ w_ _ _ _ _ _ it.

Sophie: I like to use social media to k_ _ _ u_ with my friends. Sometimes I m_ _ _ _ _ _ someone to support them if they are feeling sad.

Hannah: But a lot of c_ _ _ _ _ _ _ _ _ _ _ _ also happens online. My brother experienced it and I don't want it to happen to me.

Sophie: You can b_ _ _ _ the people who say nasty things.

Hannah: I guess so. I just want to see if I can live without social media, to be honest.

Sophie: Good luck!

7 Put the verbs in the right sentences in the right forms.

run off | go red | be sorry | point to | get on

1. She ________________ about the mess she had made in the kitchen.
2. When my father gets angry, he ________________.
3. I used to ________________ with my brother, but now we argue a lot.
4. Yesterday my dog ________________, and he still hasn't come back.
5. Please ________________ the correct answer now.

8 Which is the odd one out?

1. text message • account • cyberbullying • war
2. ancient • affair • transatlantic • complicated
3. temple • conflict • be sorry • forgive
4. additionally • apparently • misunderstanding • understandably
5. storm • leave • award • run off

Topic 2

p. 63	**politics** *(pl only)* ['pɒlətɪks]	Politik
	business ['bɪznɪs]	*hier:* Geschäftsleben
	search [sɜːtʃ]	Suche
	to **trust** [trʌst]	vertrauen
	advance [əd'vɑːns]	Fortschritt
	artificial intelligence [ˌɑːtɪˌfɪʃl‿ɪn'telɪdʒns]	künstliche Intelligenz
	to **regret** [rɪ'gret]	bedauern; bereuen
	simple ['sɪmpl]	einfach
	just [dʒʌst]	*hier:* genau(so)
	algorithm ['ælgrɪðm]	Algorithmus *(Rechenvorgang, der nach einem bestimmten Schema abläuft)*
	set of instructions [ˌset‿əv‿ɪn'strʌkʃnz]	*hier:* Befehlsfolge; Gebrauchsanweisung
	to **surf (the internet)** [ˌsɜːf (ði‿'ɪntənet)]	(durchs Internet) surfen
	to **monitor** ['mɒnɪtə]	überwachen; kontrollieren
	suitable ['suːtəbl]	geeignet; passend
	content ['kɒntent]	Inhalt
	feed [fiːd]	*hier:* (Web-)Feed; Futter; Zufuhr
	supporter [sə'pɔːtə]	Anhänger; Anhängerin; Fan
	to **enable** [ɪ'neɪbl]	befähigen; ermöglichen
	data ['deɪtə]	Daten; Angaben
	privacy *(no pl)* ['prɪvəsi]	Privatsphäre; Intimsphäre; Privatleben
	to **encounter** [ɪn'kaʊntə]	treffen; begegnen
	driverless ['draɪvələs]	führerlos; fahrerlos
	to **be said to** *(+ inf)* [bi 'sed tə]	gelten als; sollen
	efficient [ɪ'fɪʃnt]	effizient; leistungsfähig
	human being [ˌhjuːmən 'biːɪŋ]	Mensch
	monotonous [mə'nɒtnəs]	monoton; eintönig
	demanding [dɪ'mɑːndɪŋ]	anspruchsvoll; anstrengend; fordernd
	warehouse ['weəhaʊs]	Lager; Lagerhalle; Depot
	goods *(no pl)* [gʊdz]	Güter; Waren

	partially sighted [ˌpɑːʃli ˈsaɪtɪd]	sehbehindert
	assistant [əˈsɪstnt]	Assistent; Assistentin; Mitarbeiter; Mitarbeiterin
	criminal [ˈkrɪmɪnl]	Krimineller; Kriminelle; Verbrecher; Verbrecherin
p. 64	**automatically** [ˌɔːtəˈmætɪkli]	automatisch; selbsttätig
	product [ˈprɒdʌkt]	Produkt
	expert [ˈekspɜːt]	Experte; Expertin
	Japan [dʒəˈpæn]	Japan
p. 65	**streaming** [ˈstriːmɪŋ]	Streaming(-Dienst)

9 Write the words and find the train that uses AI.

1. Be careful about the ☐ _ _ _ you give away online.
2. You can put lots of goods in a big _ _ ☐ _ _ _ _ _ _.
3. Some companies _ _ _ ☐ _ _ _ everything you do online.
4. Customers have a right to data _ _ _ ☐ _ _ _.
5. A website's _ _ _ _ ☐ _ _ is more important than the design.
6. She likes to _ _ ☐ _ the web when she is bored.
7. _ _ _ _ _ _ _ ☐ _ sometimes have to go to prison.
8. A technology _ _ _ ☐ _ _ has professional knowledge of technology.
9. A ☐ _ _ _ _ _ task is easy to do.
10. Her new phone is _ _ ☐ _ as good as mine.

_ _ _ _ _ _ _ _ _ _ trains use AI.

10 Complete the table.

Infinitive	Simple past	Present perfect
1. ______	forgave	______
2. ______	______	kept up
3. leave	______	______
4. regret	______	______

11 Choose the right words.

There are lots of advantages and disadvantages to artificial intelligence. Some people think we can ______ (encounter/trust) it, but others think that robots are dangerous. Can we replace ______ (streaming/human beings) with AI?

Robots can be used in ______ (warehouses/algorithms) to complete tasks that are ______ (monotonous/expert). But AI can also be a simple set of ______ (content/instructions) that must be followed. AI is part of our everyday lives and there have been lots of ______ (advances/politics) in the last few years.

12 Find ten nouns.

G	E	A	L	G	O	R	I	T	H	M	E	D	D
S	P	S	L	A	T	B	M	F	A	Y	E	V	A
B	U	S	I	N	E	S	S	U	L	S	G	A	T
R	F	I	H	P	R	U	Y	Q	O	D	P	G	A
A	D	S	I	J	O	P	N	A	B	O	R	C	F
D	O	T	N	E	G	P	O	L	I	T	I	C	S
V	E	A	W	P	R	O	D	U	C	T	V	E	G
A	J	N	U	T	S	R	R	I	G	T	A	B	A
N	M	T	F	E	D	T	A	P	H	S	C	C	W
C	Y	C	O	N	T	E	N	T	F	O	Y	J	I
E	N	B	Z	I	K	R	E	V	I	P	T	U	N

1. ______________________

2. ______________________

3. ______________________

4. ______________________

5. ______________________

6. ______________________

7. ______________________

8. ______________________

9. ______________________

10. ______________________

Text 2

p. 67	**mystery** ['mɪstri]	Rätsel; Geheimnis
	mathematician [ˌmæθmə'tɪʃn]	Mathematiker; Mathematikerin
	unknown [ʌn'nəʊn]	unbekannt
	wartime ['wɔːtaɪm]	Kriegszeit(en); Kriegs-
	sensitive ['sensɪtɪv]	sensibel; empfindlich; verständnisvoll; vertraulich
	fascinated ['fæsɪneɪtɪd]	fasziniert
	to **imitate** ['ɪmɪteɪt]	imitieren; nachahmen
	thinking *(no pl)* ['θɪŋkɪŋ]	Denken; Überlegung; Meinung
	to **come up with sth** [ˌkʌm‿'ʌp wɪð]	sich etw. einfallen lassen; auf etw. kommen
	accurate ['ækjərət]	akkurat; genau
	to **lay the groundwork (for sth)** [ˌleɪ ðə 'graʊndwɜːk fɔː]	die Grundlagen schaffen (für etw.)
	estate [ɪ'steɪt]	Grundbesitz; Grundstück; Anwesen
	codebreaker ['kəʊdˌbreɪkə]	Codebreaker *(jmd., der einen [Geheim-]Code knackt)*
	to **decode** [ˌdiː'kəʊd]	entschlüsseln
	Nazi commander [ˌnɑːtsi kə'mɑːndə]	Nazikommandeur
	to **encrypt** [ɪn'krɪpt]	verschlüsseln
	meaningless ['miːnɪŋləs]	bedeutungslos; sinnlos
	ally ['ælaɪ]	Alliierter *(Verbündeter)*; Alliierte *(Verbündete)*
	to **intercept** [ˌɪntə'sept]	abfangen
	to **break** [breɪk]	*hier:* knacken
	to **estimate** ['estɪmeɪt]	schätzen
	via [vaɪə]	via; über
	to **test** [test]	testen; prüfen
	closely ['kləʊsli]	genau
	to **resemble** [rɪ'zembl]	ähneln
	homosexual [ˌhəʊmə'sekʃul]	Homosexueller; Homosexuelle; homosexuell

	illegal [ɪ'li:gl]	illegal; unrechtmäßig; rechtswidrig
	burglary ['bɜ:gləri]	Einbruch
	trial ['traɪəl]	Gerichtsverfahren; Gerichtsverhandlung
	no longer [ˌnəʊ 'lɒŋgə]	nicht mehr; nicht länger
	depressed [dɪ'prest]	depressiv; deprimiert; bedrückt
p. 68	**accidental** [ˌæksɪ'dentl]	versehentlich
	poisoning ['pɔɪsənɪŋ]	Vergiftung
	truth [tru:θ]	Wahrheit
	to **contribute** [kən'trɪbju:t]	beitragen; mitwirken
	enlightened [ɪn'laɪtnd]	aufgeklärt; liberal

13 Complete the text about Alan Turing.

Alan Turing's work was a m______________ to most people who knew him. He was n____ l______________ allowed to work for the government after they found out he was h____________________, because at that time it was i__________________. The t_______ is that he actually c_______ u____ with the idea of the computer, and he tried to make something that would i__________ human thinking. He became a member of a team of c_______________. They were successful in decoding the Enigma machine, which was used by the Germans to e_________ their messages.

14 Match the opposites and put the words into the sentences.

a) Match the opposites.

1. accidental	a) happy
2. fascinated	b) lies
3. truth	c) bored
4. depressed	d) known
5. unknown	e) on purpose

b) Put the words into the sentences.

1. She hadn't been feeling very ____________________ lately, even though her friends supported her. She was feeling quite ____________________.
2. My brother is ____________________ by the tigers in the zoo, but he is ____________________ of the fish, because they don't do much.
3. I just wanted to know the ____________________. I was fed up with the ____________________ that everyone was telling me.
4. Alan Turing's story was ____________________ for many years. Now, after years of research, it is ____________________.
5. The first time I got off at that train station, it was ____________________. The second time, it was ____________________, because I wanted to visit that city.

15 Find the words.

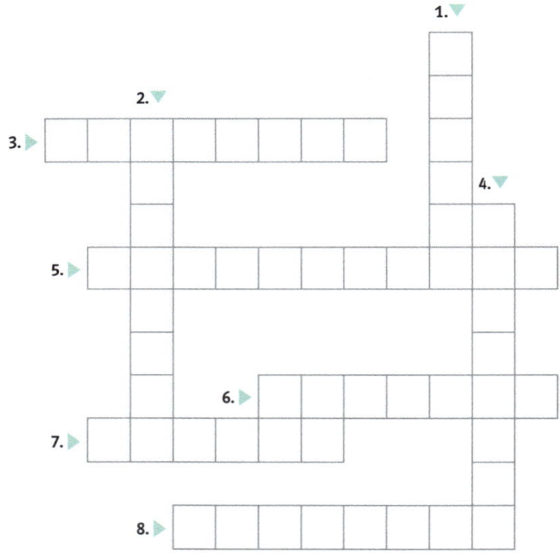

▼
1. An area of land owned by someone is an … .
2. When you … someone, you look a lot like them.
4. … is another word for guess.

▶
3. A … is when someone enters a house to steal.
5. If something doesn't have a purpose, it is … .
6. Alan Turing was awarded an OBE for his … work.
7. When you … an encrypted message, you find out its meaning.
8. If something is … , the details are correct.

Look at literature

p. 76	**comedy** ['kɒmədi]	Komödie
	tragedy ['trædʒədi]	Tragödie
	marriage ['mærɪdʒ]	Ehe; Heirat
	nonsense ['nɒnsns]	Unsinn; Quatsch
	element ['elɪmənt]	Element
p. 77	**act** [ækt]	*hier:* Akt; Handlung; Tat; Gesetz
	playwright ['pleɪraɪt]	Dramatiker; Dramatikerin
	hero *(sg)* ['hɪərəʊ], **heroes** *(pl)* ['hɪərəʊz]	Held
	scenery ['si:nri]	*hier:* Bühnenbild
	actress ['æktrəs]	Schauspielerin
	prop [prɒp]	Requisite
	female ['fi:meɪl]	weiblich
	curtain ['kɜ:tn]	Vorhang
	spectator [spek'teɪtə]	Zuschauer; Zuschauerin
	heroine ['herəʊɪn]	Heldin
	jealousy ['dʒeləsi]	Eifersucht; Neid
	hatred ['heɪtrɪd]	Hass; Abscheu
	power ['paʊə]	Energie; Kraft; Macht
	to **be in love (with)** [bi‿ɪn 'lʌv (wɪð)]	verliebt sein (in)
	at first sight [ət ˌfɜ:st 'saɪt]	auf den ersten Blick
	enemy ['enəmi]	Feind; Feindin
p. 78	**coward** [kaʊəd]	Feigling
	meanwhile [ˌmi:n'waɪl]	mittlerweile; in der Zwischenzeit
	masked ball [ˌmɑ:skt 'bɔ:l]	Maskenball
	beauty ['bju:ti]	Schönheit
p. 79	**immediately** [ɪ'mi:diətli]	sofort; gleich
	rose [rəʊz]	Rose
	sweet [swi:t]	süß
p. 80	**friar** ['fraɪə]	Bruder *(Mönch)*
	to **marry** ['mæri]	*hier:* trauen
	shortly ['ʃɔ:tli]	kurz; in Kürze; bald
	fortune ['fɔ:tʃu:n]	Schicksal

	to **banish** ['bænɪʃ]	verbannen
	cell [sel]	*hier:* Mönchszelle; Zelle
	nurse [nɜ:s]	*hier:* Amme ***(Kindermädchen)***
	ring [rɪŋ]	Ring
p. 81	**heartbroken** ['hɑ:tˌbrəʊkn]	todunglücklich; untröstlich
	count [kaʊnt]	Graf
	potion ['pəʊʃn]	Trank
	deep [di:p]	tief
	to **free** [fri:]	befreien
p. 82	**poison** ['pɔɪzn]	Gift
	kiss [kɪs]	Kuss
	dagger ['dægə]	Dolch
p. 83	to **fall in love (with)** [ˌfɔ:l‿ɪn 'lʌv]	sich verlieben (in)

1 Write the words and put them in the right sentences.

a) What do the pictures show?

1.  ____________________
2.  ____________________
3.  ____________________
4.  ____________________

b) Put the words from a) in the right sentences.

1. The __________ rises and the show begins.
2. Juliet gives Romeo a __________ as a sign of their love.
3. Juliet says that a __________ always smells sweet.
4. Juliet uses a __________ to kill herself at the end.

2 Match the opposites.

1. enemy	a) medicine
2. comedy	b) tragedy
3. poison	c) male
4. hatred	d) friend
5. female	e) love

3 Complete the text about Romeo and Juliet.

Romeo and Juliet meet at a m_ _ _ _ _ b_ _ _ and

they fall in love at f_ _ _ _ s_ _ _ _ .

They m_ _ _ _ each other secretly because their

families are enemies. Then Romeo is b_ _ _ _ _ _ _

from Verona for killing Juliet's cousin. However, the

f_ _ _ _ agrees to help them. He gives Juliet a

p_ _ _ _ _ that sends her into a d_ _ _ sleep. It

makes her seem dead. M_ _ _ _ _ _ _ _, the friar tries

to send Romeo a message but Romeo doesn't get it. He thinks

Juliet is really dead and he is so h_ _ _ _ _ _ _ _ _ _

that he kills himself. When Juliet sees that he is dead,

she i_ _ _ _ _ _ _ _ _ _ kills herself too.

4 Find eight theatre words.

R	A	S	C	E	N	E	R	Y	T
I	D	P	A	G	X	L	I	W	O
K	S	E	C	F	A	H	T	E	C
B	A	C	T	O	Z	U	R	L	U
O	W	T	G	I	M	A	A	P	R
P	L	A	Y	W	R	I	G	H	T
M	U	T	R	J	A	T	E	V	A
A	C	O	M	E	D	Y	D	H	I
V	R	R	A	K	I	W	Y	A	N
C	E	L	P	I	P	R	O	P	H

1. ______________________ 5. ______________________

2. ______________________ 6. ______________________

3. ______________________ 7. ______________________

4. ______________________ 8. ______________________

5 Which is the odd one out?

1. enemy • power • hero • coward
2. deep • heartbroken • sweet • shortly
3. beauty • immediately • nonsense • jealousy
4. friar • nurse • fortune • count

6 Find the words.

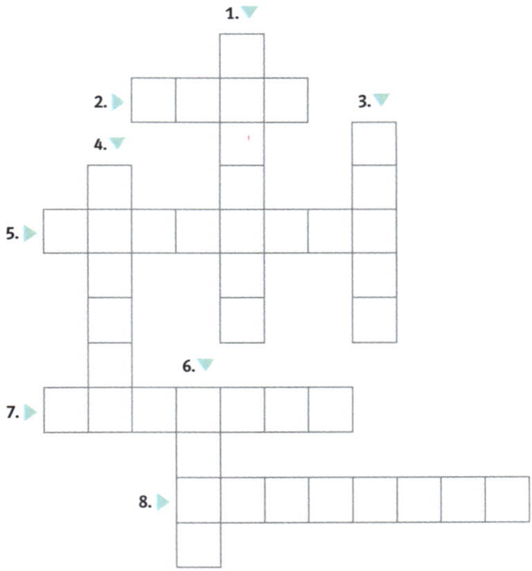

▼ 1. The main good female character in a play is the … .

3. If someone is your … , they are against you.

4. When you … someone, you send them away.

6. At a wedding you give a … to your husband/ wife.

▶ 2. When you … someone, you let them go.

5. He was very happy about his daughter's … because he liked her husband.

7. … means soon or quickly.

8. Something that doesn't make sense is … .

Unit 4 Inside India

Intro

p. 86	**contrast** ['kɒntrɑ:st]	Gegensatz; Kontrast; Unterschied
	in the country [ɪn ðə 'kʌntri]	auf dem Land
	luxury ['lʌkʃri]	Luxus(-)
	monument ['mɒnjəmənt]	Denkmal
	such as ['sʌtʃ‿əz]	wie
	poverty ['pɒvəti]	Armut
	Hindu ['hɪndu:]	Hindu; hinduistisch
	Christian ['krɪstʃn]	Christ; Christin; christlich
	Buddhist ['bʊdɪst]	Buddhist; Buddhistin; buddhistisch
	spring [sprɪŋ]	Frühling
	to **worship** ['wɜ:ʃɪp]	verehren; anbeten
	to **pray** [preɪ]	beten
p. 87	**non-violent** [ˌnɒn'vaɪəlnt]	friedlich; gewaltfrei
	call centre ['kɔ:l ˌsentə]	Callcenter
	standard ['stændəd]	Standard; Maßstab; Wertvorstellung
	wage [weɪdʒ]	Lohn
	attractive [ə'træktɪv]	attraktiv
	to **arrange** [ə'reɪndʒ]	ausmachen; arrangieren; (an)ordnen
	globalisation [ˌgləʊblaɪ'zeɪʃn]	Globalisierung
	western ['westən]	westlich
	society [sə'saɪəti]	Gesellschaft
	prince [prɪns]	Prinz
	princess [prɪn'ses]	Prinzessin

1 Complete the facts about India.

wages | spring | Hindu | contrast | western

1. Family connections are often more important in India than in ______________ societies.
2. In India there are lots of religions, but most people are ______________.
3. Holi takes place in ______________ . It is an ancient festival of colours.
4. Lots of people in India earn low ______________ for their work.
5. There is a big ______________ between the lives of the rich and the poor in India.

2 What are the words in English?

1.  _ _ _ _ _ _

2.  _ _ _ _

3.  _ _ _ _ _ _ _ _

4.  _ _ _ _ _ _ _ _ _ _

3 Find the words.

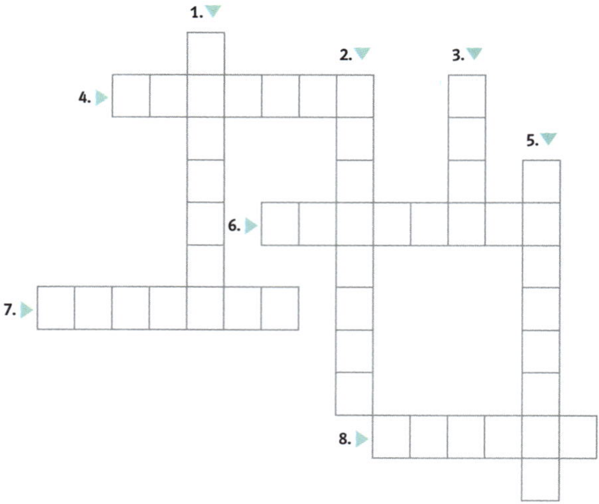

▼

1. … is another word for 'plan' or 'organise'.
2. A … is the daughter of a king and queen.
3. A regular payment for your work is a … .
5. A high … means a high level or quality.

▶

4. A church is a place where people can … their God.
6. A statue or building for a person or event is a … .
7. All the people living together in one country are a … .
8. Some people in India live in … but others are very poor.

Topic 1

p. 88	**well** [wel]	*hier:* weit
	demand [dɪˈmɑːnd]	Nachfrage; Bedarf; Verlangen
	to **provide** [prəˈvaɪd]	bieten; bereitstellen; versorgen
	to **be based** [biː ˈbeɪst]	seinen Sitz haben
	department [dɪˈpɑːtmənt]	Abteilung
	client [klaɪənt]	Klient; Klientin; Kunde; Kundin
	staffing [ˈstɑːfɪŋ]	Personalbeschaffung
	to **run** [rʌn]	*hier:* betreiben; leiten
	on site [ˌɒn ˈsaɪt]	vor Ort
	accent [ˈæksnt]	Akzent
	to **be asleep** [biː əˈsliːp]	schlafen
	individual [ˌɪndɪˈvɪdʒuəl]	Einzelperson; Individuum
	reality [riˈæləti]	Realität; Wirklichkeit
	update [ˈʌpdeɪt]	Aktualisierung
	to **crash** [kræʃ]	*hier:* abstürzen
	the Netherlands [ðə ˈneðələndz]	die Niederlande
	desk [desk]	Schreibtisch; Schalter
	to **have sth done** [ˌhæv ˌsʌmθɪŋ ˈdʌn]	etw. machen lassen
	dabbawala [ˌdæbəˈwɒlə]	Dabba-Träger *(Zusteller von Mittagessen in Mumbai)*
	delivery [dɪˈlɪvri]	Lieferung; Zustellung; Liefer-
	to **go out with** [ˌɡəʊ‿ˈaʊt wɪð]	gehen mit; ausgehen mit
p. 90	to **order** [ˈɔːdə]	bestellen
	to **repaint** [ˌriːˈpeɪnt]	neu streichen

When you learn a new word, think about how you would use it in a sentence. This helps you to understand and remember the words better!

4 Choose the right words.

Hey Daniel!

I heard you wanted to hear about my job. Well, I am a website developer and we ______________ (provide/crash) an online service that designs websites for other companies.

I love my job – I have my own ______________ (update/desk), but we don't always have to be ______________ (reality/on site); we can work from home.

I am ______________ (based/run) in the sports ______________ (department/delivery), so I design websites for sports companies. I like communicating with my ______________ (individuals/clients), but when there is too much ______________ (order/demand), I have to work very long hours.

Speak to you soon!

Maybe I can hear about your job then too 😊

5 Match the opposites.

1. asleep	a) group
2. reality	b) ugly
3. wealth	c) dream
4. individual	d) awake
5. attractive	e) poverty

6 Write in the words and find the name of a popular service in Mumbai.

1. ☐_ _ _ _ _ _ _ services transport goods from one place to another.
2. Apps on old mobile phones often _ _☐_ _ , which means they suddenly stop working.
3. A result of _ _ _☐_ _ _ _ _ _ _ _ _ is that different parts of the world become more connected and businesses become more international.
4. The Bank of India is an example of a big Indian company ☐_ _ _ _ in Mumbai.
5. You should try to keep up with a computer's regular _ _ _☐_ _ _ so that it continues to work.
6. There are ☐_ _ _ over 15 million people living in Mumbai.
7. Our company is very good at _ _☐_ _ _ _ _ – we only hire the best people.
8. We treat our _☐_ _ _ _ _ with respect, because they are our customers.
9. I should _ _ _☐_ _ _ the building – I want it to be a different colour.

_ _ _ _ _ _ _ _ _ is a person who delivers lunchboxes to people at work.

Topic 2

p. 95	**regret** [rɪ'gret]	Bedauern; Reue
	to **have a crush on sb** [ˌhæv‿ə 'krʌʃ‿ɒn]	in jmdn. verknallt sein; auf jmdn. stehen
	headset ['hedset]	Kopfhörer; Headset
	a while [ə 'waɪl]	eine Weile
	to **fetch** [fetʃ]	(ab)holen
	to **hand sb sth** [hænd]	jmdm. etw. (über)reichen
	torture ['tɔːtʃə]	Folter; Qual
	in a whisper [ɪn‿ə 'wɪspə]	leise; flüsternd
	in secret [ɪn 'siːkrət]	im Geheimen; insgeheim
	before long [bɪˌfɔː 'lɒŋ]	in Kürze; recht bald
	furious ['fjʊəriəs]	wütend
	to **ruin** ['ruːɪn]	ruinieren; zerstören
	to **threaten** ['θretn]	(be)drohen
	option ['ɒpʃn]	Möglichkeit; Option; Wahl
	drastic ['dræstɪk]	drastisch; einschneidend
p. 96	**commando** [kə'mɑːndəʊ]	Kommando; Angehörige(r) eines Kommandotrupps
	lawyer ['lɔɪə]	Anwalt; Anwältin; Jurist; Juristin
	activist ['æktɪvɪst]	Aktivist; Aktivistin *(jmd., der sich für etw. engagiert)*
	mission ['mɪʃn]	Mission; Auftrag
	couple ['kʌpl]	Paar
	helpline ['helplaɪn]	Notruf; telefonische Beratung
	safety ['seɪfti]	Sicherheit
	point [pɔɪnt]	*hier:* Zweck
p. 97	**as far as ... is concerned** [əz ˌfɑːr‿əz ... ɪz kən'sɜːnd]	Was ... angeht ...
	honesty ['ɒnɪsti]	Ehrlichkeit
	responsibility [rɪˌspɒnsə'bɪləti]	Verantwortung
	alcohol *(no pl)* ['ælkəhɒl]	Alkohol
	to **take off** [ˌteɪk‿'ɒf]	ausziehen; abnehmen
	in public [ɪn 'pʌblɪk]	in der Öffentlichkeit; öffentlich

7 Complete the dialogue.

rjsafetyneawhiletzfuriousrncouplekjconcernedscoptionsnalawyerpusecretlm

Avni: Hey Dhruv! Don't you think Afshan and Sanchit are a cute ______________?

Dhruv: Yes! Did you know that they are getting married in ______________? Their parents don't know.

Avni: Really? Why?

Dhruv: Well, Afshan is a Muslim, and Sanchit is a Hindu. Their parents would be ______________ if they found out.

Avni: Oh no. They have been together for a ______________. Do they have any other ______________?

Dhruv: Maybe they could leave India. They might need a ______________ to help them.

Avni: I think that their ______________ is the most important thing.

Dhruv: I agree. As far as I am ______________, religion should not keep people apart.

8 Match the words with their definitions.

1. activist	a) an important task
2. torture	b) a telephone service that gives advice
3. helpline	c) a person who works to change something
4. mission	d) feeling sad or disappointed
5. regret	e) causing someone pain on purpose

9 Put the verbs in the right sentences in the right forms.

hand | threaten | take off | fetch | ruin

1. I was drawing a nice picture when my brother ________________ it.
2. Today in the park I ________________ my coat because it was so warm.
3. Last night, his parents ________________ to take away his phone.
4. Please ________________ me your passport – I have to look at the photo.
5. My dog likes to ________________ my shoes.

10 What can you see in the pictures?

1. ______________________
2. ______________________
3. ______________________
4. ______________________

11 Which is the odd one out?

1. threaten • mission • fetch • ruin
2. responsibility • happiness • helpline • honesty
3. couple • lawyer • activist • commando
4. attractive • furious • threaten • drastic

12 Write the words in the table.

heartbroken option furious headset

take off fetch safety sweet forgive

Nouns	Verbs	Adjectives

Text 2

p. 99	**file** [faɪl]	*hier:* Akte; Mappe; Datei
	obituary [ə'bɪtʃʊəri]	Traueranzeige; Nachruf
	fanatic [fə'nætɪk]	Fanatiker; Fanatikerin; fanatisch
	to **confront** [kən'frʌnt]	konfrontieren; entgegentreten; sich stellen
	violence *(no pl)* ['vaɪəlns]	Gewalt
	glasses *(pl)* ['glɑːsɪz]	Brille
	to **break** [breɪk]	*hier:* verstoßen gegen
	soul [səʊl]	Seele
	average ['ævrɪdʒ]	durchschnittlich
	law [lɔː]	*hier:* Jura
	guard [gɑːd]	*hier:* Zugbegleiter(in); Wache; Wächter; Wächterin
	colonial [kə'ləʊniəl]	kolonial; Kolonial-
	campaign [kæm'peɪn]	Kampagne; Aktion
	oppression [ə'preʃn]	Unterdrückung
	speech [spiːtʃ]	Sprache; Rede
	to **resist** [rɪ'zɪst]	sich widersetzen; widerstehen
	peaceful ['piːsfl]	friedlich
	to **boycott** ['bɔɪkɒt]	boykottieren
	to **go on a hunger strike** [ˌgəʊ ɒn‿ə 'hʌŋgə ˌstraɪk]	in (einen) Hungerstreik treten
	increase ['ɪnkriːs]	Zunahme; Wachstum; Anstieg
	victim ['vɪktɪm]	Opfer
p. 100	**basic** ['beɪsɪk]	grundlegend; einfach; Grund-
	message ['mesɪdʒ]	*hier:* Botschaft
	march [mɑːtʃ]	Marsch; Kundgebung
	to **stand up for sth** [ˌstænd‿'ʌp fə]	sich einsetzen für
p. 101	**not even** [ˌnɒt‿'iːvn]	(noch) nicht einmal
	injustice [ɪn'dʒʌstɪs]	Ungerechtigkeit
	none [nʌn]	keine; keiner; keines
	nearby [ˌnɪə'baɪ]	in der Nähe; nahe gelegen
p. 102	**Sikh** [siːk]	Sikh

rule [ruːl]	*hier:* Herrschaft
to **divide (into)** [dɪˈvaɪd]	teilen; aufteilen; unterteilen
extremist [ɪkˈstriːmɪst]	radikal; extremistisch; Extremist; Extremistin
to **act** [ækt]	*hier:* handeln
principle [ˈprɪnsəpl]	Prinzip; Grundsatz
murder [ˈmɜːdə]	Mord
to **envisage** [ɪnˈvɪzɪdʒ]	sich vorstellen
to **establish** [ɪˈstæblɪʃ]	gründen; einrichten; eröffnen
equal [ˈiːkwəl]	gleich; gleichberechtigt
master [ˈmɑːstə]	Meister; Herr
struggle [ˈstrʌgl]	Kampf; Anstrengung
engaged (in) [ɪnˈgeɪdʒd]	beteiligt (an); besetzt; belegt
to **end up** [ˌend‿ˈʌp]	enden; landen
blind [blaɪnd]	blind

13 Match the words with their definitions.

1. someone who has unusually strong political or religious views	a) victim
2. someone who watches and protects a person or place	b) march
3. when lots of people walk together to protest against something	c) extremist
4. someone who is injured or killed because of a crime or an accident	d) obituary
5. something you write about someone after their death	e) guard

14 Complete the text about Gandhi.

Mahatma Gandhi was killed on 30th January 1948. He was killed by a Hindu f______________ who felt Gandhi's attitude to Muslims was too friendly. The m______________ happened at Birla House in Bombay, where Gandhi was pr______________. People will remember Mahatma Gandhi as the father of no______________ protest. He tried to end the op______________ of India by the British and won. Gandhi was born on 2nd October 1869. At the age of 18, he moved to London to study l__________. After university, he worked as a l______________ in South Africa, where he experienced a lot of di__________________ because of his skin colour. In South Africa, Gandhi fought for the rights of thousands of Indians who worked for the British go______________ there. He continued fighting for civil r__________ when he returned to India. In his sp______________ Gandhi asked people to join him in his peaceful protest. He asked them to bo______________ everything that was British: the courts, the schools and even the English language. He was very brave for fighting against in______________ without using violence.

15 Find the words.

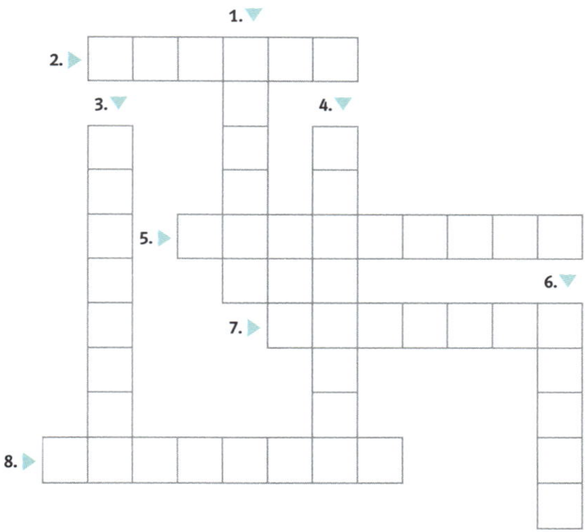

▼

1. If you … something, you stand up against it.
3. When you come face to face with something, you … it.
4. … means without violence.
6. When people have the same rights and opportunities, they are … .

▶

2. … means close, or not far away.
5. When you … a company, you create and begin it.
7. A … is the main point made in a speech, film etc.
8. A fight to break free, or a conflict, is a … .

Zoom in – The Commonwealth

1 monarch, organisation, New Zealand, aims, climate change, sporting event, disability, recent

2 1. b, 2. e, 3. d, 4. c, 5. a

Unit 1 – Life down under

Intro

3 1. continent, 2. Australian, 3. lifestyle, 4. Aboriginal, 5. diseases, 6. Agriculture, 7. koala → outback

4 contact, down under, koalas, kangaroos, education, these days, housing

Topic 1

5 1. b, 2. d, 3. c, 4. e, 5. a

6 ignorant, giant, skilled, daily, sacred, respectful, nomadic, common

7 1. koala, 2. kangaroo, 3. lady (woman), 4. plant

8 1. knowledge, 2. respectful, 3. connection, 4. behaviour, 5. tolerate, beliefs, 6. ignore, 7. accept

Topic 2

9 mentioned, No way, Aussie, loads of, barbies, Speaking of, mates

10 nouns: trip, harbour, seashell, decoration
verbs: mention, communicate, gleam, depend
adjectives: laid-back, brilliant, honest, jealous

11 1. look up, 2. work out, 3. pass on, 4. walk by, 5. put on

12 1. coral, 2. creature, 3. left, 4. honest

13 1. trip, 2. honest, 3. lady, 4. harbour, 5. mention, 6. gleam, 7. sacred, 8. frightened, 9. plant → Indonesia

Text 2

14 1. snorkelling, 2. turtle, 3. coral

15 destination, lanes, consequences, repair, recover, polluted, ecosystem, government

16 b) 1. government, 2. ecosystem, 3. waste, 4. platform, 5. consequence, 6. destination, 7. earth, 8. stress

Unit 2 – The world of work

Intro

1 a) 1. chef, 2. travel agent, 3. (hair) stylist, 4. nurse
b) 1. chef, restaurant, 2. travel agent, agency, 3. (hair) stylist, salon, 4. nurse, hospital

2 1. apprentice, 2. workplace, 3. shift, 4. tiring, 5. ecosystem

3 agent, colleagues, understanding, specialise, work, tiring, workplace, advantages, shifts

Topic 1

4 excellent, prepared, progress, salary, abroad, requirements, photography, detail, grades, driving licence, apply

5 1. d, 2. c, 3. f, 4. a, 5. b, 6. e

6 1. d, 2. e, 3. b, 4. a, 5. c

Topic 2

7 apprenticeship, advert, CV, volunteered, typed, qualified, sincerely

8 qualified, confident, determined, attached, deaf, intermediate, advanced, everyday

9 1. pilot, 2. piano, 3. surgeon, 4. duck

10 letter of application, reference, hard-working, applying, repairs, qualifications, grade, secondary, interview

Text 2

11 1. d, 2. b, 3. a, 4. e, 5. c

12 ▼ 1. secret, 3. payment, 5. mint, 6. useful
▶ 2. exchange, 4. currency, 7. introduction, 8. virtual (digital)

13 currency, coins, credit card, payment, secure, balance, make sure, treat, fool

Unit 3 – Our digital lives

Intro

1 1. revolutionised, 2. spread, 3. represented, 4. carried, 5. published

2 1. medal, 2. lip, 3. temple, 4. (homing) pigeon

3 1. human, 2. crisis, 3. emojis, 4. war, 5. tomb, 6. grain, 7. lips, 8. copy, 9. publish, 10. throughout → hieroglyph

Topic 1

4 1. b, 2. d, 3. f, 4. a, 5. c, 6. e

5 nouns: conflict, misunderstanding, affair, account
verbs: shorten, delete, forgive, inform
adjectives: transatlantic, complicated, certain, ancient

6 message, account, on purpose, do without, keep up, message, cyberbullying, block

7 1. was sorry, 2. goes red, 3. get on, 4. ran off, 5. point to

8 1. war, 2. affair, 3. temple, 4. misunderstanding, 5. award

Topic 2

9 1. data, 2. warehouse, 3. monitor, 4. privacy, 5. content, 6. surf, 7. Criminals, 8. expert, 9. simple, 10. just
→ driverless

10 1. forgive, forgiven, 2. keep up, kept up, 3. left, left, 4. regretted, regretted

11 trust, human beings, warehouses, monotonous, instructions, advances

12 algorithm, business, politics, product, content, advance, assistant, supporter, privacy, data

Text 2

13 mystery, no longer, homosexual, illegal, truth, came up, imitate, codebreakers, encrypt

14 a) 1. e, 2. c, 3. b, 4. a, 5. d

b) 1. happy, depressed, 2. fascinated, bored, 3. truth, lies, 4. unknown, known, 5. accidental, on purpose

15 ▼ 1. estate, 2. resemble, 4. estimate

▶ 3. burglary, 5. meaningless, 6. wartime, 7. decode, 8. accurate

Look at literature

1 a) 1. dagger, 2. ring, 3. curtain, 4. rose

b) 1. curtain, 2. ring, 3. rose, 4. dagger

2 1. d, 2. b, 3. a, 4. e, 5. c

3 masked ball, first sight, marry, banished, friar, potion, deep, Meanwhile, heartbroken, immediately

4 scenery, act, playwright, comedy, prop, spectator, tragedy, curtain

5 1. power, 2. shortly, 3. immediately, 4. fortune

6 ▼ 1. heroine, 3. enemy, 4. banish, 6. ring

▶ 2. free, 5. marriage, 7. shortly, 8. nonsense

Unit 4 – Inside India

Intro

1 1. western, 2. Hindu, 3. spring, 4. wages, 5. contrast

2 1. prince, 2. pray, 3. princess, 4. call centre

3 ▼ 1. arrange, 2. princess, 3. wage, 5. standard
▶ 4. worship, 6. monument, 7. society, 8. luxury

Topic 1

4 provide, desk, on site, based, department, clients, demand

5 1. d, 2. c, 3. e, 4. a, 5. b

6 1. delivery, 2. crash, 3. globalisation, 4. based, 5. updates, 6. well, 7. staffing, 8. clients, 9. repaint → dabbawala

Topic 2

7 couple, secret, furious, while, options, lawyer, safety, concerned

8 1. c, 2. e, 3. b, 4. a, 5. d

9 1. ruined, 2. took off, 3. threatened, 4. hand, 5. fetch

10 1. alcohol, 2. headset, 3. desk, 4. couple

11 1. mission, 2. helpline, 3. couple, 4. threaten

12 nouns: option, headset, safety
verbs: take off, fetch, forgive
adjectives: heartbroken, furious, sweet

Text 2

13 1. c, 2. e, 3. b, 4. a, 5. d

14 fanatic, murder, praying, non-violent, oppression, law, lawyer, discrimination, government, rights, speeches, boycott, injustice

15 ▼ 1. resist, 3. confront, 4. peaceful, 6. equal
▶ 2. nearby, 5. establish, 7. message, 8. struggle